796.357
RAM   Rambeck, Richard
       Oakland Athletics

25657

DATE DUE	BORROWER'S NAME
2 88020	Michael Iboyt

25657   Oakland Athletics

796.357
RAM   Rambeck, Richard
       Oakland Athletics

TORRINGFORD SCHOOL MEDIA

OAKLAND
ATHLETICS

AL WEST

RICHARD RAMBECK

Published by Creative Education, Inc.

123 S. Broad Street, Mankato, Minnesota 56001

Art Director, Rita Marshall
Cover and title page design by Virginia Evans
Cover and title page illustration by Rob Day
Type set by FinalCopy Electronic Publishing
Book design by Rita Marshall

Photos by Duomo, Focus on Sports, Sportschrome, UPI/Bettmann and Wide World Photos

Library of Congress Cataloging-in-Publication Data

Rambeck, Richard.

  Oakland Athletics / by Richard Rambeck.

  p. cm.

  Summary: A team history of the "A's," born in
Philadelphia, resident in Kansas City, and now settled
in Oakland, where for twenty years they have been
highly successful.

  ISBN 0-88682-444-3

  1. Oakland Athletics (Baseball team)—History—
Juvenile literature. [1 Oakland Athletics (Baseball
team)—History. 2. Baseball—History.] I. Title.
GV875.O24R36 1991   91-10139
796.357'64'0979466—dc20   CIP

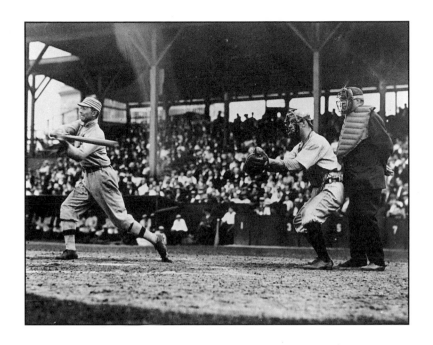

THE EARLY YEARS

Perhaps the city of Oakland would be better known if it weren't just across the bay from San Francisco. Many consider San Francisco to be the most beautiful and cosmopolitan of major U.S. cities. Oakland, however, is also a thriving city, a West Coast hub of railroad transportation. Called the "Jewel of the East Bay," Oakland was founded in 1854 on the eastern shore of San Francisco Bay, and the city began to grow rapidly in the wake of the California gold rush.

By 1900 there were more than sixty thousand residents in Oakland; today the population has grown to more than 350,000. The east bay city is much more spread out than its neighbor to the west: San Francisco, which has more than twice the population of Oakland, is actually eight

All-time Athletic great Home Run Baker.

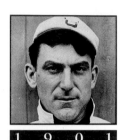

*Hall-of-Famer Nap
Lajoie hit .422 and
won the AL's Triple
Crown in the
league's first season.*

square miles smaller. The pace of life in Oakland is less hectic than it is in San Francisco. Even the wind, for which San Francisco is famous, is much more mild in Oakland.

Oakland city officials have always striven to assure that their city is not lost in the shadow of San Francisco. While San Francisco is rich in cultural history, the city of Oakland has a professional sports tradition that is at least equal, if not superior, to that of San Francisco. A major part of Oakland's sports tradition is its professional baseball team, the Athletics, one of the most successful franchises in the major leagues during the last two decades.

The Athletics, or A's as they often are known, have won nine American League West Division titles, six league pennants, and four World Series championships in the last twenty years. No other major-league team has claimed as many division titles or World Series victories in as short a timespan. The story of the Athletics franchise is one of success, but it is also one of failure. It is also a tale of three cities: The Athletics were born almost three thousand miles from Oakland, in Philadelphia, and also spent time in Kansas City.

The driving force behind the formation of the Phila-delphia Athletics in 1901 was Cornelius McGillicuddy, a man whose name was shortened—although no one was sure why—to Connie Mack. Mack bought 25 percent of the team, which was one of the charter members of the new American League. He was an owner and the team's manager for an amazing fifty years. Mack led the Athletics to nine American League pennants and five World Series titles during his tenure.

The driving force behind today's Athletics, Jose Canseco.

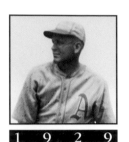

1 9 2 9

Howard Ehmke set a World Series record by striking out 13 batters in the opening victory over Chicago.

Philadelphia dominated the American League from 1910 to 1914, winnning four pennants in five years. The team was built around the fabulous talents of a pair of hard-hitting infielders: Eddie Collins and Frank "Home Run" Baker. Unfortunately, Connie Mack's penny-pinching ways soon got the team in trouble. The problems began when a new baseball league—the Federal League, which didn't last long—was formed in 1913. The Federal League offered much higher salaries to players in the American and National League who would leave their teams and join clubs in the new league. Most American League and National League teams kept their stars by matching the offers of Federal League clubs, but Connie Mack refused to do this. The Athletics lost star pitchers Charles Albert "Chief" Bender and Eddie Plank to the Federal League, and as a result, suffered a talent shortage that would hurt the club for more than ten years.

Mack managed to rebuild the team by the mid-1920s. At the end of that decade, Philadelphia once again had risen to the top of the American League. The Athletics had a collection of great hitters, including Al Simmons, Jimmie Foxx, catcher Mickey Cochrane, and Bing Miller. They also had quality pitching, thanks to Lefty Grove, George Earnshaw, and George "Rube" Walberg.

These stars rocketed the Athletics to three straight American League pennants from 1929 to 1931, and World Series titles in 1929 and 1930. After winning the 1931 pennant, though, the team was never able to recapture its glory days while in Philadelphia, or in Kansas City, where the franchise moved in 1955. In fact, from 1935 to 1967, the Athletics finished no higher than fourth in the American League. In the thirteen years the team spent in Kansas City, the A's never finished higher than sixth in the league.

The biggest news the Kansas City Athletics ever made was when the team changed owners in December 1960. Charles O. Finley paid $1.9 million for 52 percent of the club. Two months later Finley, who was known throughout his colorful reign as Charlie O., bought the remaining 48 percent for another $1.9 million. Finley, was a wealthy man, and he was used to getting his way. He was creative, stubborn, and confident. Although he insulted his managers, coaches, and players, he eventually built the A's into the best team in baseball. In fact, the Athletics became only the second franchise in major-league history—the other was the New York Yankees—to win three straight World Series championships.

The A's moved to Kansas City and finished sixth in the league under manager Lou Boudreau.

FINLEY HOOKS CATFISH

Although Finley would move the team to Oakland in 1968, he began building the club's championship roster while still in Kansas City. In 1962 he signed shortstop Bert Campaneris as a free agent. Two years later pitcher Jim "Catfish" Hunter joined the team. Catcher Gene Tenace, outfielder Joe Rudi, and relief pitcher Rollie Fingers came aboard in 1965. That same year Finley drafted and signed outfielder Rick Monday and third baseman Sal Bando. Slugging outfielder Reggie Jackson was selected in the 1966 draft, and hard-throwing pitcher Vida Blue was drafted a year later.

In 1968, the year the A's moved from Kansas City to Oakland, Hunter served notice to the rest of the

9

Another slugging Athletic, Dave Henderson.

The magical Dennis Eckersley.

The storied career of Jim "Catfish" Hunter (right) began in Kansas City.

American League that he was a star on the rise. He did so by throwing the first regular-season perfect game by an American League pitcher in forty-six years in a contest against the hard-hitting Minnesota Twins. He allowed no hits, no walks, and no one reached base.

Hunter's biggest asset was his ability to put the ball where he wanted it. His excellent control was the result of years of practice. "I always had a baseball in my hand growing up," Hunter recalled. "I watched my brother Pete pitch, and I watched baseball on television. I've always had real good control, although it's been better the last three or four years. Even in high school, I tried to hit the corners."

Hunter was also a calm, cool presence in the locker room, a constant inspiration to his teammates. "He always impressed me as a kid who had it all together," said veteran third baseman Ed Charles. "He was a wholesome character to have on the team. He was always in control of himself."

Led by Hunter's heroics, the Oakland A's finished sixth in the ten-team American League in 1968. A year later the club wound up with eighty-eight victories—and only seventy-four losses—to finish second in the AL West Division. (In 1969 the American League expanded from ten to twelve teams and was divided into two divisions: the East and West.)

All-Star shortstop Bert Campaneris led the team in hits, runs, at-bats and triples.

JACKSON JUMPS TO CENTER STAGE

The improving A's were a big story in 1969, but the hitting of Reggie Jackson was an even bigger sensation. For much of the season, Jackson hit home runs at a pace that matched that of Roger Maris when he set the major-league single-season record of sixty-one homers. The pressure on the young slugger became incredible; he was the biggest fan attraction in the majors. Jackson eventually tailed off and finished the year with forty-seven homers, a total that was second in the league to that of Minnesota's Harmon Killebrew.

Jackson had become perhaps the most feared long-ball hitter in the American League. "When you hit a terrific shot," Jackson said, "all the baseball players come to rest at that moment and watch you. Everyone is helpless and in awe. You charge people up by hitting the long ball. And when you're a good hitter, you do that every day. You're the center of confidence. 'The man can hit,' they say. And you *know* it. You're a master. There's no feeling like that."

Oakland third baseman Sal Bando set a club record by earning 118 walks.

Jackson, however, fell into an awful slump in 1970, when he batted just .237 with twenty-three home runs and sixty-six RBI. "I'm trying, really trying," Jackson exclaimed during the season. "Maybe too hard. But the slump has made me a better person. You learn to be a man all over again."

The Oakland power hitter also learned how to keep his teammates loose even when he was struggling. "He has a sense of humor about it," said one Oakland player of Jackson's slump. "He's dying inside, but do you know what he did when we left Anaheim? He went around offering to take care of the luggage. He saluted for an imaginary tip, just like a red cap. I had to laugh. It was kind of funny, you know. I mean, he didn't sulk or quit."

Jackson and the A's wound up second in the AL West in 1970—a good finish, but not good enough for demanding owner Charlie Finley. He fired manager John McNamara and replaced him with Dick Williams, who had led the Boston Red Sox from nowhere in 1966 to the top of the American League in 1967. Williams knew what it took to win championships, something the Athletics franchise hadn't done in forty years.

In 1971, everything finally began to fall into place for the club. Young pitcher Vida Blue put together a dream season. He lost his first decision and then won the next ten in a row to lead the A's into first place. Blue wound up the year with twenty-four victories, a 1.82 earned-run average, and 301 strikeouts, all of which topped the American League. For his efforts Blue was named the American League's Cy Young Award winner, as well as its Most Valuable Player. Blue and other Oakland pitchers got plenty of support from Reggie Jackson (thirty-two

Ace lefthander Vida Blue (right) struck out a club record 17 batters in a game against California.

home runs), Sal Bando (twenty-four home runs), and first baseman Mike Epstein (nineteen home runs).

Oakland won the AL West with an amazing 101–60 record, but the team's luck ran out in the league championship series. Oakland lost to the Baltimore Orioles in the best-of-five series, allowing the Orioles to advance to their third straight World Series. The A's had put together the franchise's best year since 1931, but the team was still disappointed. There would, however, be no disappointments the next three years. Before the 1972 season, Finley traded outfielder Rick Monday to the Chicago Cubs for pitcher Ken Holtzman. It proved to be a very important move. The A's needed a little more pitching to put them over the top, and Holtzman gave the team a solid third starter to back up Catfish Hunter and Vida Blue.

Oakland roared to its second straight AL West title and then defeated the Detroit Tigers in the league championship series. For the first time in forty-one years, the A's were in the World Series. The experts gave the team little chance to defeat Cincinnati's powerful "Big Red Machine," especially since Reggie Jackson was injured and would miss the series. But the A's shocked the baseball world by defeating the Reds four games to three. The big reason for the upset was the hitting of catcher Gene Tenace, who had gone only one for seventeen against Detroit in the American League Championship Series. In the World Series, Tenace blasted four home runs, had nine RBI, and batted .348 to win the Most Valuable Player award.

The A's colorful owner, Charlie Finley, was named "The Sporting News" Sportsman of the Year.

After winning the 1972 World Series, the A's coasted to the 1973 AL West title behind Reggie Jackson, who led the American League in homers (thirty-two) and RBI (117), and was named the league's Most Valuable Player. Oakland then defeated Baltimore to advance to the World Series for the second straight year. For Reggie Jackson, playing in the World Series was something new; he had missed the 1972 series and vowed to make the most of his chance in 1973. Jackson didn't disappoint the Oakland fans. Behind his hitting, the A's defeated the New York Mets four games to three, and Jackson was named MVP.

Despite the team's success, Dick Williams stepped down as manager. He was tired of Finley's unpredictable antics. Finley replaced Williams with Alvin Dark, who managed the A's once before, when they were in Kansas City. This time Dark had more success, and the powerful A's rolled to their fourth straight division title and third

Seventeen years later (1990), Rickey Henderson led Oakland to another world championship (pages 18–19).

1 9 7 4

For the third consecutive season Reggie Jackson (right) was selected as a starter in the All-Star Game.

consecutive American League pennant, beating Baltimore again in the league championship series.

The hero in 1974 for the A's was Catfish Hunter, who posted the lowest earned-run average in the American League and was honored with the Cy Young Award. In the World Series, however, another Oakland pitcher stood at center stage. Reliever Rollie Fingers was named the Most Valuable Player as Oakland defeated the Los Angeles Dodgers four games to one.

The victory over the Dodgers allowed the A's to become only the second team in major-league history to win three straight World Series titles, and there was every reason to believe their success would continue. However, it didn't. The A's entered the 1975 season without Catfish Hunter, who had become a free agent and signed with the New York Yankees. Oakland still managed to win their fifth straight division title in 1975, but they lost in the league championship series to the Boston Red Sox. Soon they also lost most of their other stars, as Finley either traded them or allowed them to become free agents and sign with other teams. Perhaps the most bitter pill for Oakland fans to swallow was the trading of Reggie Jackson to Baltimore.

The A's quickly went from the top to the bottom of the American League West, and the Oakland fans soon lost interest in the team. Finley finally lost interest in being an owner in 1979, and sold the last-place A's to a group led by Walter J. Haas, Jr. After this, changes came quickly. Roy Eisenhardt was named club president, and his first move was hiring Billy Martin to manage the team.

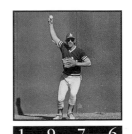

Oakland outfielder Joe Rudi won his second Gold Glove award in three years.

Under Martin's direction, the A's of 1980 were transformed from a doormat to a contender. Outfielder Tony Armas slammed thirty-five homers and drove in 109 runs, and Rickey Henderson, another outfielder, stole an American League record one hundred bases. In addition, Oakland's starting pitchers completed ninety-four of 162 games, an American League record that may never be broken.

The A's recaptured the hearts of their fans, who started trooping back to Oakland Alameda County Coliseum to watch what everyone was calling "Billyball." After two years of continued improvement, the A's won the 1982 AL West title, but then lost in the league championship series to the New York Yankees. Ironically, the Yanks were led by Reggie Jackson and Catfish Hunter. That was last anyone heard of Billyball in Oakland. In 1983 Oakland starting pitchers Mike Norris, Rick Langford, and Steve McCatty all developed arm trouble, which many

An Oakland star of the late 1980s, Dave Stewart.

believed was a result of Martin having overworked them. The A's posted their worst record in fourteen years, and Martin resigned.

By the mid-1980s the A's were still struggling to regain their championship form. Steve Boros and Jackie Moore were both hired and fired as Oakland managers. After Moore was canned in the middle of the 1986 season, the A's hired Tony La Russa, who led the Chicago White Sox to the American League West Division title in 1983. La Russa inherited a team that was long on ability but a little short on confidence. He worked to instill that confidence, and he also showed faith in certain players whom other managers might have given up on. One of these was a pitcher named Dave Stewart.

1 9 8 4

For the third consecutive year Athletics' outfielder Rickey Henderson was named to the AL All-Star team.

STEWART MAKES HIS PITCH FOR GREATNESS

In the first game La Russa managed with the A's, Dave Stewart, who had been inconsistent throughout his major-league career, got the victory. For the rest of the 1986 season, Stewart was the hottest pitcher in the American League, posting a 9–1 record. The experts were convinced that Stewart, who had been a disappointment with both the Los Angeles Dodgers and Texas Rangers, would fall on his face in 1987. But he didn't; in fact, he won twenty games, almost twice as many as he had won in any previous season in the majors. Stewart's success shocked almost everyone in baseball—including Stewart. "I've really been trying to concentrate on the ball club and the pennant race," Stewart said late in the 1987 season. "But now that the season is coming to an end, I'm starting to realize that, hey, I've really had a

Left to right: Stan Javier, Mike Moore, Bob Welch, Walt Weiss.

good year. I'd never even dreamed of winning twenty games. I knew that if I got the chance, I could be a good pitcher, but . . . . Anyway, I won't dwell on it until it's all over."

Stewart didn't dwell on his success, but his teammates and coaches did, and they wondered when their ace starter would receive the credit they thought he had earned. "I've never seen anyone who was so consistent," said Oakland pitching coach Dave Duncan. "He takes the same stuff to the mound every start, and every time he starts, the A's think they're going to win."

Stewart and the A's came up just short in the AL West race in 1987, losing out to the Minnesota Twins. But there was no stopping Oakland in 1988, and there was no stopping powerful right fielder Jose Canseco, who was voted the American League's Most Valuable Player. Canseco, who led the league in homers with forty-two, became the first major-league player to hit at least forty homers and steal at least forty bases in a season. The man who was the American League Rookie of the Year in 1986 had become perhaps the most complete player in the game.

"There's so much talk about his power that people overlook the work he's done to correct his limitations," said Jim Lefebvre, manager of the Seattle Mariners and former Oakland batting coach. "He's spent hours working on his [batting] stroke, on his concentration, his patience at the plate." Canseco's manager, La Russa, also praised Canseco's work habits. I don't think the average person has any idea of the amount of effort that goes into the kind of play he's giving us," La Russa said. "And I don't mean just hitting. I'm looking at the whole

In his first season as manager Tony LaRussa predicts a world championship "in five years or less."

All-Star catcher Terry Steinbach (pages 26–27).   25

Shortstop Walt Weiss was named AL Rookie of the Year in recognition of his fine overall play.

package—his defense, his base running. He plays this game intelligently."

Led by Canseco, the A's almost went all the way in 1988. They won 104 games to claim the AL West Division title and then defeated the Boston Red Sox four games to none in the American League Championship Series. The Athletics were the heavy favorites to beat the Los Angeles Dodgers in the World Series. However, Oakland star relief pitcher Dennis Eckersley gave up a dramatic ninth-inning homer to L.A.'s Kirk Gibson in the first game that gave the Dodgers a 5–4 victory. The A's never recovered from that blow, nor did they find their hitting strokes against Los Angeles pitching. The Dodgers won the series four games to one.

After their disappointment in the 1988 series, the A's rebounded to win another division title in 1989, despite the fact that Canseco missed almost half the season with an injury. Dave Stewart posted his third straight twenty-win season, and first baseman Mark McGwire, outfielder Dave Henderson, and designated hitter Dave Parker made up for any power shortage caused by Canseco's absence. Oakland then defeated Toronto four games to one in the league championship series and advanced to play cross-bay rival San Francisco in the World Series.

In the series, Stewart and Mike Moore held the power-hitting Giants to only one run in the first two games, both of which the A's won easily. Then, when the series shifted to San Francisco's Candlestick Park for game three, the entire Bay Area was rocked by a devastating earthquake. The series was postponed, and then resumed more than a week later. Oakland's bats could not be silenced in games three and four, and the A's wound

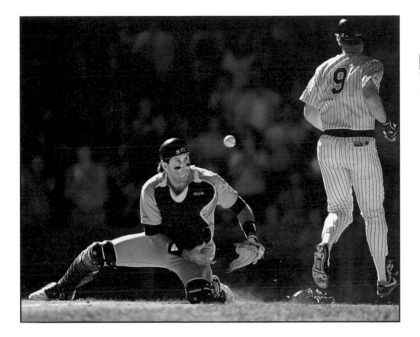

Back-up catcher Ron Hassey (left) completed his third season in an Oakland uniform.

up sweeping the series four games to none. Stewart, who won twice in the series, was named the Most Valuable Player.

The A's almost duplicated their 1989 success the following season. Pitcher Bob Welch won an amazing twenty-seven games, the most victories by any major-league pitcher in eighteen years. Stewart won twenty-two games for the A's, who claimed another division title and posted a record of 103–59, the best win-loss mark in baseball. Most experts expected Oakland to roll to another World Series championship.

After sweeping the Boston Red Sox four games to none in the American League Championship Series, Oakland was favored to defeat the Cincinnati Reds in the World Series. The Reds, however, used strong pitching and timely hitting to take four straight games from the

First baseman Mark McGwire.

Third baseman Carney Lansford.

1 9 9 1

The slick fielding and home run phenom Mark McGwire continued his All-Star play.

surprised A's. Oakland had to settle for second-best for the second time in three years.

Despite their defeat in the 1990 World Series, the A's remain the dominant team in the American League. The club has young stars such as Canseco, Mark McGwire, catcher Terry Steinbach, and shorstop Walt Weiss. It also has veteran standouts such as Rickey Henderson, who was trade by the New York Yankees back to Oakland in 1989, plus pitchers Dave Stewart, Mike Moore, Bob Welch, and Dennis Eckersley.

Some experts are even comparing the current A's team with the squad that won three straight World Series titles in the early 1970s. The present team has one advantage over the club of almost twenty years ago; the newer version of the A's doesn't have to contend with the antics of an unpredictable owner like Charlie Finley. Finley's A's, however, did win three straight championships, an achievement the current team would do well to equal.